What are Seventh-day Adventists?

Seventh-day Adventists are a denomination within the Christian protestant movement. We accept the Bible as our only creed and hold certain fundamental beliefs from the teachings of the Holy Scriptures. These 28 core beliefs are based 100% on the Bible's teaching and we test everything we believe again⟨…⟩ the Bible. When something we believe can not ⟨…⟩ will gladly accept it to be false.

The reader of this book is, however, encouraged ⟨…⟩ not blindly believe what is being said in this book. Conduct your own research and Bible study. Look at what the Bible says and study the text of the Bible. This is one of the ways in which you can get to know God and who God is.

I hope you enjoy this Seventh-day Adventist Bible study guide and fully comprehend the plan God has for you and this world. I hope you see the bigger picture and God's immeasurable loved for us through the study of the Bible.

Number 1: The Holy Scriptures

The Holy Scriptures, Old and New Testaments, are the written Word of God, given by divine inspiration. The inspired authors spoke and wrote as they were moved by the Holy Spirit. In this Word, God has committed to humanity the knowledge necessary for salvation. The Holy Scriptures are the supreme, authoritative, and the infallible revelation of His will. The Bible shares it's view of God's Character. God is Love. This again, ties with the concept that the Bible must guide you in what you believe. The Bible is the supreme authority in every way and must be believed above the word of any man.

Write down the essence of these Verses:

Psalms 119:105:

Proverbs 30:5, 6:

Isaiah 8:20:

John 17:17:

1 Thessalonians 2:13:

2 Timothy 3:16, 17:

Hebrews 4:12; 2:

Peter 1:20, 2:

Number 2: The Holy Trinity

There is one God: Father, Son, and Holy Spirit, a unity of three coeternal Persons. God is immortal, all-powerful, all-knowing, above all, and ever present. He is infinite and beyond human comprehension, yet known through His self-revelation. God, **who is love**, is forever worthy of worship, adoration, and service by the whole creation.

Something to remember: It is often difficult to understand this concept: How can 3 beings be 1? Visualise yourself in a team with 3 players. All of the 3 players essentially want to win the game and for that moment, their goals, wishes and hopes are aligned. That is exactly how God can be three beings, yet one. They have the same goals, wishes, hopes and character. They are 3 independent beings, but essentially have the exact same "personality" and therefore are 1.

Write down the meaning of these verses:

Genesis 1:26:

Deuteronomy 6:4:

Isaiah 6:8:

Matthew 28:19:

John 3:16

2 Corinthians 1:21, 22; 13:14

Ephesians 4:4-6

1 Peter 1:2:

<u>Notes</u>

Number 3: God the Father

God the eternal Father is the Creator, Source, Sustainer, and Sovereign of all creation. He is just and holy, merciful and gracious, slow to anger, and abounding in steadfast love and faithfulness. The qualities and powers exhibited in the Son and the Holy Spirit are also those of the Father.

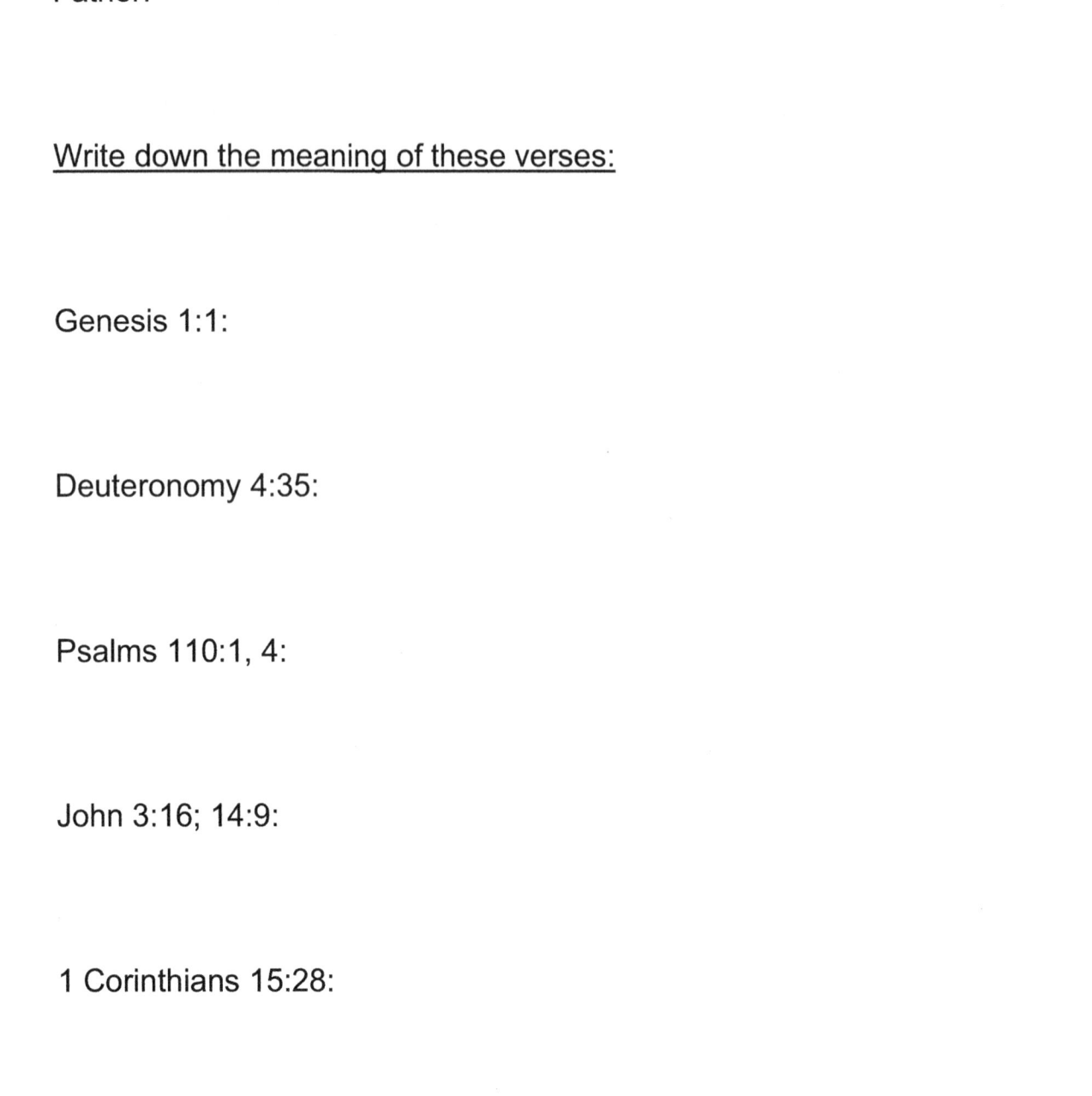

Write down the meaning of these verses:

Genesis 1:1:

Deuteronomy 4:35:

Psalms 110:1, 4:

John 3:16; 14:9:

1 Corinthians 15:28:

1 Timothy 1:17:

1 John 4:8:

Revelation 4:11:

Notes

Number 4: God the Son

God the eternal Son became incarnate in Jesus Christ. Through Him all things were created, the character of God is revealed, the salvation of humanity is accomplished, and the world is judged. Forever truly God, He became also truly human, Jesus the Christ. He was conceived of the Holy Spirit and born of the virgin Mary. He lived and experienced temptation as a human being, but perfectly exemplified the righteousness and love of God. By His miracles He manifested God's power and was attested as God's promised Messiah. He suffered and died voluntarily on the cross for our sins and in our place, was raised from the dead, and ascended to heaven to minister in the heavenly sanctuary in our behalf. He will come again in glory for the final deliverance of His people and the restoration of all things.

Write down the meaning of these verses:

Isaiah 53:4-6:

Daniel 9:25-27:

Luke 1:35:

John 1:1-3 14; 5:22; 10:30; 14:1-3, 9, 13;

Romans 6:23:

1 Cor. 15:3, 4; 2:

Philliphians 2:5-11:

Hebrews 2:9- 18; 8:1, 2:

Notes:

Number 5: God the Holy Spirit

God the eternal Spirit was active with the Father and the Son in Creation, incarnation, and redemption. He is as much a person as are the Father and the Son. He inspired the writers of Scripture. He filled Christ's life with power. He draws and convicts human beings; and those who respond He renews and transforms into the image of God. Sent by the Father and the Son to be always with His children, He extends spiritual gifts to the church, empowers it to bear witness to Christ, and in harmony with the Scriptures leads it into all truth.

Write down the meaning of these verses:

Genesis 1:1, 2:

2 Samuel 23:2:

Psalms 51:11:

Isaiah 61:1:

Luke 1:35; 4:18:

John 14:16-18, 26; 15:26:

Acts 1:8; 5:3; 10:38:

Romans 5:5:

1 Corinthians 12:7-11:

2 Corinthians 3:18:

2 Peter 1:21

Notes:

Number 6: Creation of the Universe

God has revealed in Scripture the authentic and historical account of His creative activity. He created the universe, and in a recent six-day creation the Lord made "the heavens and the earth, the sea, and all that is in them" and rested on the seventh day. Thus, He established the Sabbath as a perpetual memorial of the work He performed and completed during six literal days that together with the Sabbath constituted the same unit of time that we call a week today. The first man and woman were made in the image of God as the crowning work of Creation, given dominion over the world, and charged with responsibility to care for it. When the world was finished it was "very good," declaring the glory of God.

Write down the meaning of these verses:

Genesis 1-2; 5; 11:

Exodus 20:8-11:

Psalms 19:1-6; 33:6, 9; 104:

Isaiah 45:12, 18:

Acts 17:24:

Colossense 1:16:

Hebrew 1:2; 11:3:

Revelation 10:6; 14:7:

Notes:

Number 7: The Nature of Humanity

Man and woman were made in the image of God with individuality, the power and freedom to think and to do. Though created free beings, each is an indivisible unity of body, mind, and spirit, dependent upon God for life and breath and all else. When our first parents disobeyed God, they denied their dependence upon Him and fell from their high position. The image of God in them was marred and they became subject to death. Their descendants share this fallen nature and its consequences. They are born with weaknesses and tendencies to evil. But God in Christ reconciled the world to Himself and by His Spirit restores in penitent mortals the image of their Maker. Created for the glory of God, they are called to love Him and one another, and to care for their environment.

Write down the meaning of these verses:

Genesis 1:26-28; 2:7, 15; 3:

Psalms 8:4-8; 51:5, 10; 58:3:

Jeremiah 17:9:

Acts 17:24-28:

Romans 5:12-17:

2 Corinthians 5:19, 20:

Ephesians 2:3; 1

Thessalonians 5:23:

1 John 3:4 4:7, 8, 11, 20:

Notes:

Number 8: The Great Controversy

All humanity is now involved in a great controversy between Christ and Satan regarding the character of God, His law, and His sovereignty over the universe. This conflict originated in heaven when a created being, endowed with freedom of choice, in self-exaltation became Satan, God's adversary, and led into rebellion a portion of the angels. He introduced the spirit of rebellion into this world when he led Adam and Eve into sin. This human sin resulted in the distortion of the image of God in humanity, the disordering of the created world, and its eventual devastation at the time of the global flood, as presented in the historical account of Genesis 1-11. Observed by the whole creation, this world became the arena of the universal conflict, out of which the God of love will ultimately be vindicated. To assist His people in this controversy, Christ sends the Holy Spirit and the loyal angels to guide, protect, and sustain them in the way of salvation.

Write down the meaning of these verses:

Genesis. 3; 6-8:

Job 1:6-12:

Isaiah 14:12-14

Ezekiel 28:12-18

Romans 1:19-32; 3:4; 5:12-21; 8:19-22:

1 Corinthians 4:9:

Hebrews 1:14:

1 Peter 5:8:

2 Peter 3:6:

Rev. 12:4-9:

Notes:

Number 9: The life, death and resurrection of Christ

In Christ's life of perfect obedience to God's will, His suffering, death, and resurrection, God provided the only means of atonement for human sin, so that those who by faith accept this atonement may have eternal life, and the whole creation may better understand the infinite and holy love of the Creator. This perfect atonement vindicates the righteousness of God's law and the graciousness of His character; for it both condemns our sin and provides for our forgiveness. The death of Christ is substitutionary and expiatory, reconciling and transforming. The bodily resurrection of Christ proclaims God's triumph over the forces of evil, and for those who accept the atonement assures their final victory over sin and death. It declares the Lordship of Jesus Christ, before whom every knee in heaven and on earth will bow.

Write down the meanings of these verses:

Genesis 3:15:

Psalms. 22:1

Isaiah 53:

John 3:16: 14:30:

Romans 1:4; 3:25; 4:25; 8:3, 4:

1 Corinthians 15:3, 4, 20-22:

2 Cor. 5:14, 15, 19-21:

Philliphians 2:6-11:

Colossense 2:15:

1 Peter 2:21, 22:

1 John 2:2; 4:10:

Notes:

Number 10: The Experience of Salvation

In infinite love and mercy God made Christ, who knew no sin, to be sin for us, so that in Him we might be made the righteousness of God. Led by the Holy Spirit we sense our need, acknowledge our sinfulness, repent of our transgressions, and exercise faith in Jesus as Saviour and Lord, Substitute and Example. This saving faith comes through the divine power of the Word and is the gift of God's grace. Through Christ we are justified, adopted as God's sons and daughters, and delivered from the lordship of sin. Through the Spirit we are born again and sanctified; the Spirit renews our minds, writes God's law of love in our hearts, and we are given the power to live a holy life. Abiding in Him we become partakers of the divine nature and have the assurance of salvation now and in the judgment.

Write down the meaning of these verses:

Isa. 45:22; 53:

Jer. 31:31-34:

Ezekiel 33:11; 36:25-27:

Habakuk 2:4:

Mark 9:23, 24:

John 3:3-8, 16; 16:8:

Romans 3:21-26; 8:1-4, 14-17; 5:6-10; 10:17; 12:2:

2 Cor. 5:17-21:

Gal. 1:4; 3:13, 14, 26; 4:4-7;

Eph. 2:4-10:

Col. 1:13, 14:

Titus 3:3-7:

Heb. 8:7-12:

1 Peter 1:23; 2:21, 22:

2 Peter 1:3, 4:

Rev. 13:8:

Notes:

Number 11: Growing In Christ

By His death on the cross Jesus triumphed over the forces of evil. He who subjugated the demonic spirits during His earthly ministry has broken their power and made certain their ultimate doom. Jesus' victory gives us victory over the evil forces that still seek to control us, as we walk with Him in peace, joy, and assurance of His love. Now the Holy Spirit dwells within us and empowers us. Continually committed to Jesus as our Saviour and Lord, we are set free from the burden of our past deeds. No longer do we live in the darkness, fear of evil powers, ignorance, and meaninglessness of our former way of life. In this new freedom in Jesus, we are called to grow into the likeness of His character, communing with Him daily in prayer, feeding on His Word, meditating on it and on His providence, singing His praises, gathering together for worship, and participating in the mission of the Church. We are also called to follow Christ's example by compassionately ministering to the physical, mental, social, emotional, and spiritual needs of humanity. As we give ourselves in loving service to those around us and in witnessing to His salvation, His constant presence with us through the Spirit transforms every moment and every task into a spiritual experience.

Write down the meaning of these verses

1 Chronicles 29:11:

Psalms. 1:1, 2; 23:4; 77:11, 12:

Matthew 20:25-28; 25:31-46:

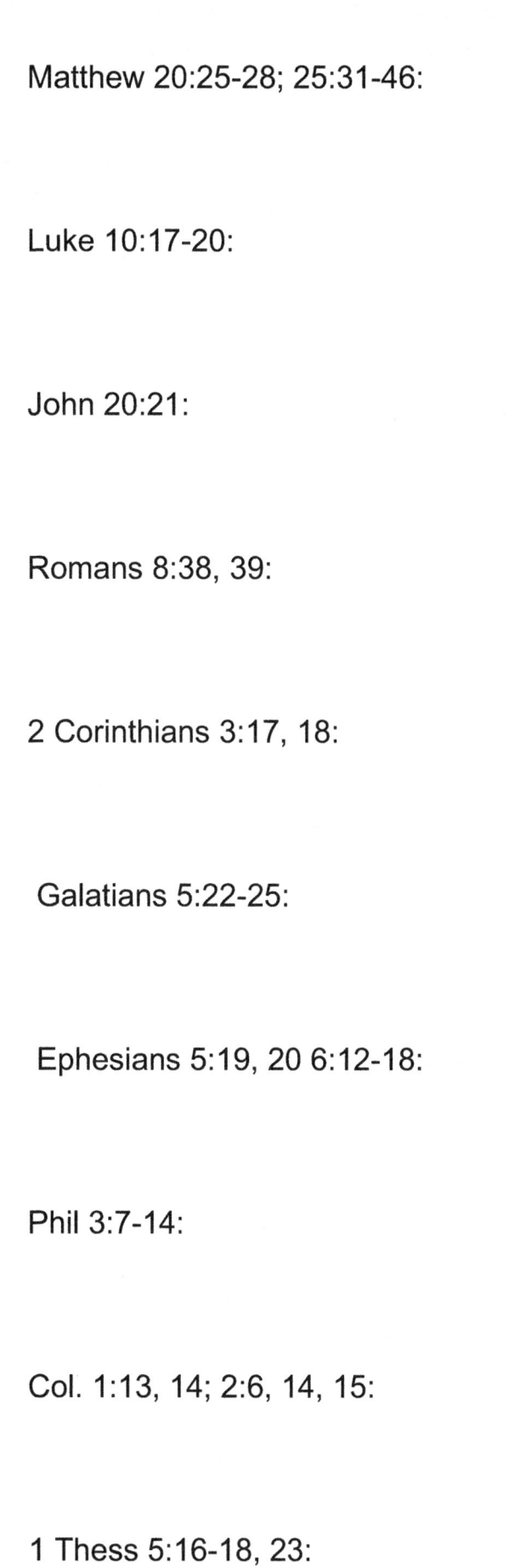

Luke 10:17-20:

John 20:21:

Romans 8:38, 39:

2 Corinthians 3:17, 18:

Galatians 5:22-25:

Ephesians 5:19, 20 6:12-18:

Phil 3:7-14:

Col. 1:13, 14; 2:6, 14, 15:

1 Thess 5:16-18, 23:

Hebrew 10:25:

James 1:27:

2 Peter 2:9; 3:18

1 John 4:4:

Notes:

Number 12: The Church

The church is the community of believers who confess Jesus Christ as Lord and Saviour. In continuity with the people of God in Old Testament times, we are called out from the world; and we join together for worship, for fellowship, for instruction in the Word, for the celebration of the Lord's Supper, for service to humanity, and for the worldwide proclamation of the gospel. The church derives its authority from Christ, who is the incarnate Word revealed in the Scriptures. The church is God's family; adopted by Him as children, its members live on the basis of the new covenant. The church is the body of Christ, a community of faith of which Christ Himself is the Head. The church is the bride for whom Christ died that He might sanctify and cleanse her. At His return in triumph, He will present her to Himself a glorious church, the faithful of all the ages, the purchase of His blood, not having spot or wrinkle, but holy and without blemish.

Write down the meaning of these verses:

Genesis 12:1-3:

Exodus 19:3-7:

Mathew 16:13-20; 18:18; 28:19, 20:

Acts 2:38-42; 7:38:

1 Cor. 1:2:

Eph. 1:22, 23: 2:19-22; 3:8-11; 5:23-27:

Col. 1:17, 18:

1 Peter 2:9:

Notes:

Number 13: The Remnant and its Mission

The universal church is composed of all who truly believe in Christ, but in the last days, a time of widespread apostasy, a remnant has been called out to keep the commandments of God and the faith of Jesus. This remnant announces the arrival of the judgment hour, proclaims salvation through Christ, and heralds the approach of His second advent. This proclamation is symbolized by the three angels of Revelation 14; it coincides with the work of judgment in heaven and results in a work of repentance and reform on earth. Every believer is called to have a personal part in this worldwide witness.

Write down the meaning if these verses:

Dan. 7:9-14:

Isa. 1:9; 11:11:

Jer. 23:3:

Mic. 2:12:

2 Cor. 5:10:

1 Peter 1:16-19; 4:17:

2 Peter 3:10-14

Jude 3, 14:

Rev. 12:17; 14:6-12; 18:1-4:

Notes:

Number 14: Unity in the Body of Christ

The church is one body with many members, called from every nation, kindred, tongue, and people. In Christ we are a new creation; distinctions of race, culture, learning, and nationality, and differences between high and low, rich and poor, male and female, must not be divisive among us. We are all equal in Christ, who by one Spirit has bonded us into one fellowship with Him and with one another; we are to serve and be served without partiality or reservation. Through the revelation of Jesus Christ in the Scriptures we share the same faith and hope and reach out in one witness to all. This unity has its source in the oneness of the triune God, who has adopted us as His children.

Write down the meaning of these verses:

Psalms 133:1

Matt. 28:19, 20:

John 17:20-23:

Acts 17:26, 27:

Rom. 12:4, 5

1 Cor. 12:12-14:

2 Cor. 5:16, 17:

Gal. 3:27-29:

Eph. 2:13-16; 4:3-6, 11-16:

Col. 3:10-15:

Notes:

Number 15: Baptism

By baptism we confess our faith in the death and resurrection of Jesus Christ, and testify of our death to sin and of our purpose to walk in newness of life. Thus, we acknowledge Christ as Lord and Saviour, become His people, and are received as members by His church. Baptism is a symbol of our union with Christ, the forgiveness of our sins, and our reception of the Holy Spirit. It is by immersion in water and is contingent on an affirmation of faith in Jesus and evidence of repentance of sin. It follows instruction in the Holy Scriptures and acceptance of their teachings.

Write down the meaning of these verses:

Matt. 28:19, 20:

Acts 2:38; 16:30-33; 22:16:

Rom. 6:1-6:

Gal. 3:27:

Col. 2:12, 13:

Notes:

Number 16: The Lord's Supper

The Lord's Supper is a participation in the emblems of the body and blood of Jesus as an expression of faith in Him, our Lord and Saviour. In this experience of communion Christ is present to meet and strengthen His people. As we partake, we joyfully proclaim the Lord's death until He comes again. Preparation for the Supper includes self-examination, repentance, and confession. The Master ordained the service of foot-washing to signify renewed cleansing, to express a willingness to serve one another in Christlike humility, and to unite our hearts in love. The communion service is open to all believing Christians.

Write down the meaning of these verses:

Matthew 26:17-30:

John 6:48-63; 13:1-17:

1 Corinthians 10:16, 17; 11:23-30

Revelation 3:20:

Notes:

Number 17: Spiritual Gifts and Ministries

God bestows upon all members of His church in every age spiritual gifts that each member is to employ in loving ministry for the common good of the church and of humanity. Given by the agency of the Holy Spirit, who apportions to each member as He wills, the gifts provide all abilities and ministries needed by the church to fulfil its divinely ordained functions. According to the Scriptures, these gifts include such ministries as faith, healing, prophecy, proclamation, teaching, administration, reconciliation, compassion, and self-sacrificing service and charity for the help and encouragement of people. Some members are called of God and endowed by the Spirit for functions recognized by the church in pastoral, evangelistic, and teaching ministries particularly needed to equip the members for service, to build up the church to spiritual maturity, and to foster unity of the faith and knowledge of God. When members employ these spiritual gifts as faithful stewards of God's varied grace, the church is protected from the destructive influence of false doctrine, grows with a growth that is from God, and is built up in faith and love.

Write down what these verses mean:

Acts 6:1-7:

Romans 12:4-8:

1 Corinthians 12:7-11, 27, 28:

Ephesians 4:8, 11-16:

1 Timothy 3:1-13:

1 Peter 4:10, 11:

Notes:

Number 18: The Gift of Prophecy

The Scriptures testify that one of the gifts of the Holy Spirit is prophecy. This gift is an identifying mark of the remnant church and we believe it was manifested in the ministry of Ellen G. White. Her writings speak with prophetic authority and provide comfort, guidance, instruction, and correction to the church. They also make clear that the Bible is the standard by which all teaching and experience must be tested.

Study and interpret the following verses:

Numbers 12:6:

2 Chronicles 20:20:

Amos 3:7:

Joel 2:28, 29:

Acts 2:14-21:

2 Tim. 3:16, 17:

Heb. 1:1-3:

Rev. 12:17; 19:10; 22:8, 9:

Notes:

Number 19: The Law of God

The great principles of God's law are embodied in the Ten Commandments and exemplified in the life of Christ. They express God's love, will, and purposes concerning human conduct and relationships and are binding upon all people in every age. These precepts are the basis of God's covenant with His people and the standard in God's judgment. Through the agency of the Holy Spirit they point out sin and awaken a sense of need for a Saviour. Salvation is all of grace and not of works, and its fruit is obedience to the Commandments. This obedience develops Christian character and results in a sense of well-being. It is evidence of our love for the Lord and our concern for our fellow human beings. The obedience of faith demonstrates the power of Christ to transform lives, and therefore strengthens Christian witness.

Study and interpret the following verses:

Exodus 20:1-17:

Deuteronomy 28:1- 14:

Psalms 19:7-14; 40:7, 8:

Matthew 5:17-20 22; 36-40:

John 14:15; 15:7-10:

Romans 8:3, 4:

Ephesians 2:8-10:

Hebrews 8:8-10:

1 John 2:3; 5:3:

Revelation 12:17; 14:12:

Notes:

Number 20: The Sabbath

The gracious Creator, after the six days of Creation, rested on the seventh day and instituted the Sabbath for all people as a memorial of Creation. The fourth commandment of God's unchangeable law requires the observance of this seventh-day Sabbath as the day of rest, worship, and ministry in harmony with the teaching and practice of Jesus, the Lord of the Sabbath. The Sabbath is a day of delightful communion with God and one another. It is a symbol of our redemption in Christ, a sign of our sanctification, a token of our allegiance, and a foretaste of our eternal future in God's kingdom. The Sabbath is God's perpetual sign of His eternal covenant between Him and His people. Joyful observance of this holy time from evening to evening, sunset to sunset, is a celebration of God's creative and redemptive acts.

Study and interpret the following verses:

Genesis 2:1-3:

Exodus 20:8-11; 31:13-17:

Leviticus 23:32:

Deuteronomy 5:12-15:

Isaiah 56:5, 6; 58:13, 14:

Ezekiel 20:12, 20:

Matthew 12:1-12:

Mark 1:32:

Luke 4:16:

Hebrews 4:1-11:

Notes:

Number 21: Stewardship

We are God's stewards, entrusted by Him with time and opportunities, abilities and possessions, and the blessings of the earth and its resources. We are responsible to Him for their proper use. We acknowledge God's ownership by faithful service to Him and our fellow human beings, and by returning tithe and giving offerings for the proclamation of His gospel and the support and growth of His church. Stewardship is a privilege given to us by God for nurture in love and the victory over selfishness and covetousness. Stewards rejoice in the blessings that come to others as a result of their faithfulness.

Study and interpret the following verses:

Gen. 1:26-28; 2:15:

1 Chron. 29:14:

Haggai 1:3-11:

Malachi 3:8-12:

Matthew 23:23:

Romans 15:26, 27:

1 Corinthians 9:9-14:

2 Corinthians 8:1-15; 9:7:

Notes:

Number 22: Christian Behavior

We are called to be a godly people who think, feel, and act in harmony with biblical principles in all aspects of personal and social life. For the Spirit to recreate in us the character of our Lord we involve ourselves only in those things that will produce Christlike purity, health, and joy in our lives. This means that our amusement and entertainment should meet the highest standards of Christian taste and beauty. While recognizing cultural differences, our dress is to be simple, modest, and neat, befitting those whose true beauty does not consist of outward adornment but in the imperishable ornament of a gentle and quiet spirit. It also means that because our bodies are the temples of the Holy Spirit, we are to care for them intelligently. Along with adequate exercise and rest, we are to adopt the most healthful diet possible and abstain from the unclean foods identified in the Scriptures. Since alcoholic beverages, tobacco, and the irresponsible use of drugs and narcotics are harmful to our bodies, we are to abstain from them as well. Instead, we are to engage in whatever brings our thoughts and bodies into the discipline of Christ, who desires our wholesomeness, joy, and goodness.

Study and interpret these verses:

Genesis 7:2:

Exodus 20:15:

Leviticus 11:1-47:

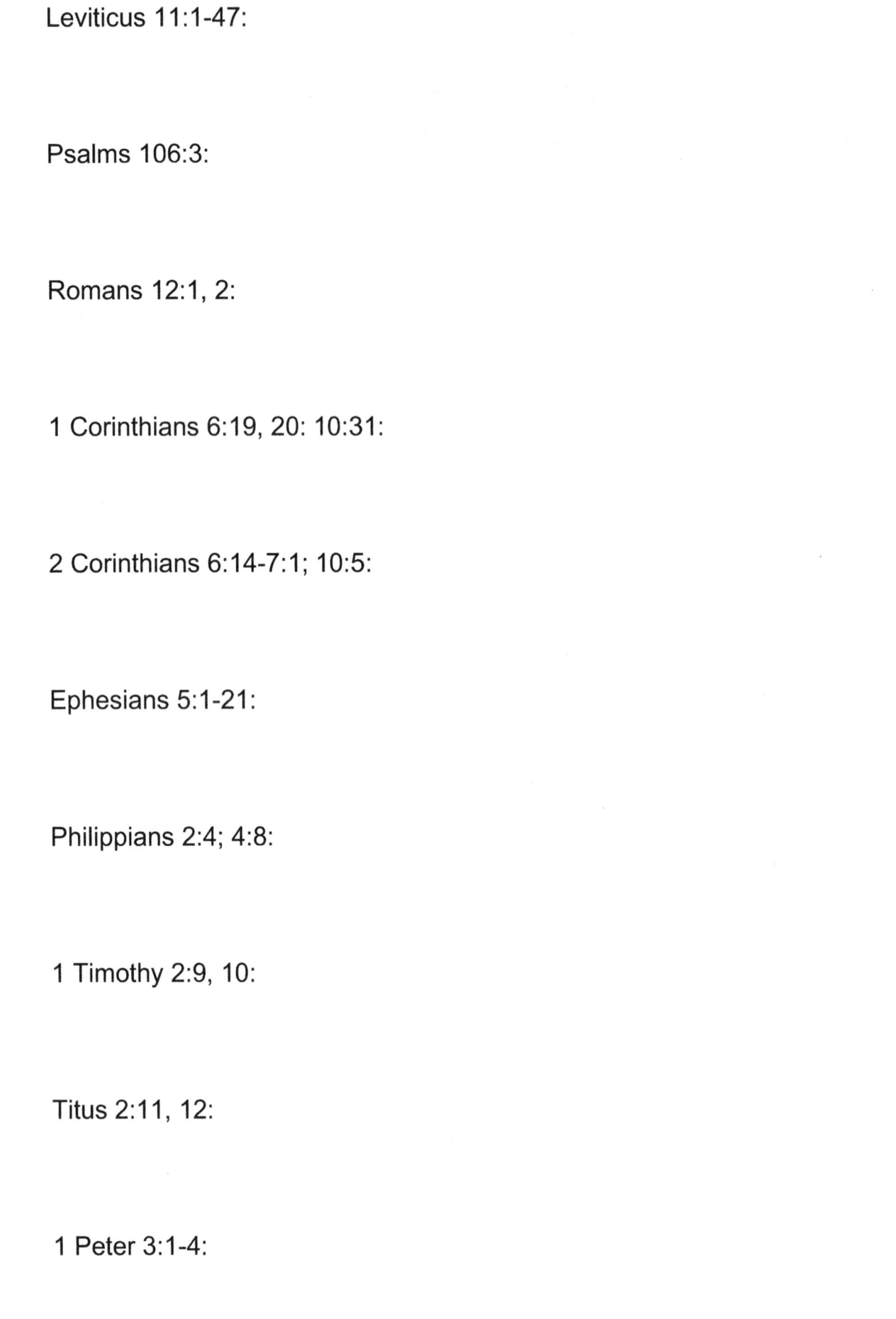

Psalms 106:3:

Romans 12:1, 2:

1 Corinthians 6:19, 20: 10:31:

2 Corinthians 6:14-7:1; 10:5:

Ephesians 5:1-21:

Philippians 2:4; 4:8:

1 Timothy 2:9, 10:

Titus 2:11, 12:

1 Peter 3:1-4:

1 John 2:6:

3 John 2:

Notes:

Number 23: Marriage and the Family

We are called to be a godly people who think, feel, and act in harmony with biblical principles in all aspects of personal and social life. For the Spirit to recreate in us the character of our Lord we involve ourselves only in those things that will produce Christlike purity, health, and joy in our lives. This means that our amusement and entertainment should meet the highest standards of Christian taste and beauty. While recognizing cultural differences, our dress is to be simple, modest, and neat, befitting those whose true beauty does not consist of outward adornment but in the imperishable ornament of a gentle and quiet spirit. It also means that because our bodies are the temples of the Holy Spirit, we are to care for them intelligently. Along with adequate exercise and rest, we are to adopt the most healthful diet possible and abstain from the unclean foods identified in the Scriptures. Since alcoholic beverages, tobacco, and the irresponsible use of drugs and narcotics are harmful to our bodies, we are to abstain from them as well. Instead, we are to engage in whatever brings our thoughts and bodies into the discipline of Christ, who desires our wholesomeness, joy, and goodness.

Study and interpret the following Verses:

Genesis 7:2:

Exodus 20:15:

Leviticus 11:1-47:

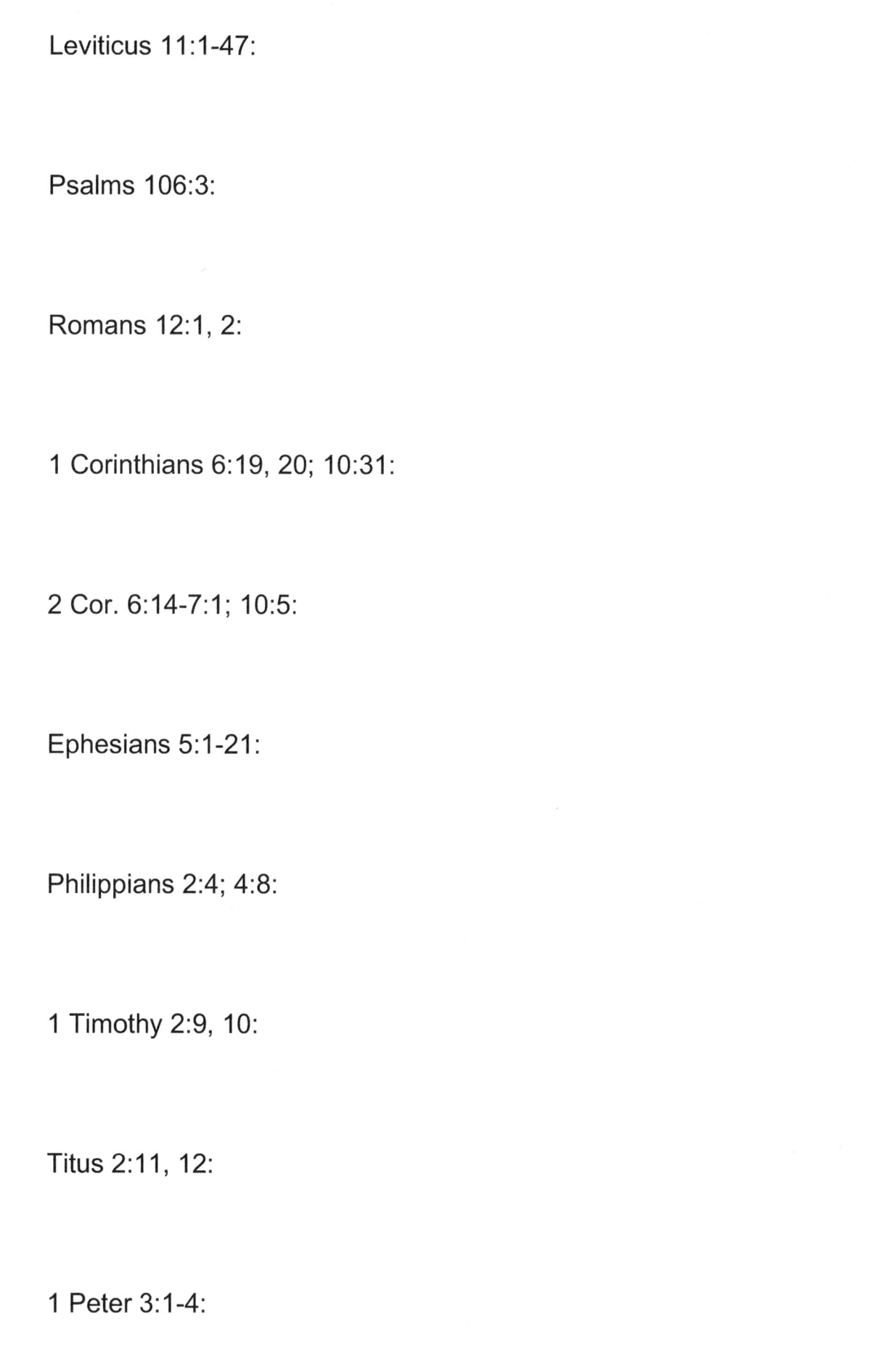

Psalms 106:3:

Romans 12:1, 2:

1 Corinthians 6:19, 20; 10:31:

2 Cor. 6:14-7:1; 10:5:

Ephesians 5:1-21:

Philippians 2:4; 4:8:

1 Timothy 2:9, 10:

Titus 2:11, 12:

1 Peter 3:1-4:

1 John 2:6:

3 John 2:

Notes:

Number 24: Christ's Ministry in the Heavenly Sanctuary

There is a sanctuary in heaven, the true tabernacle that the Lord set up and not humans. In it Christ ministers on our behalf, making available to believers the benefits of His atoning sacrifice offered once for all on the cross. At His ascension, He was inaugurated as our great High Priest and, began His intercessory ministry, which was typified by the work of the high priest in the holy place of the earthly sanctuary. In 1844, at the end of the prophetic period of 2300 days, He entered the second and last phase of His atoning ministry, which was typified by the work of the high priest in the most holy place of the earthly sanctuary. It is a work of investigative judgment which is part of the ultimate disposition of all sin, typified by the cleansing of the ancient Hebrew sanctuary on the Day of Atonement. In that typical service the sanctuary was cleansed with the blood of animal sacrifices, but the heavenly things are purified with the perfect sacrifice of the blood of Jesus. The investigative judgment reveals to heavenly intelligences who among the dead are asleep in Christ and therefore, in Him, are deemed worthy to have part in the first resurrection. It also makes manifest who among the living are abiding in Christ, keeping the commandments of God and the faith of Jesus, and in Him, therefore, are ready for translation into His everlasting kingdom. This judgment vindicates the justice of God in saving those who believe in Jesus. It declares that those who have remained loyal to God shall receive the kingdom. The completion of this ministry of Christ will mark the close of human probation before the Second Advent.

Study and interpret these verses:

Leviticus 16:

Numbers 14:34:

Ezekiel 4:6:

Daniel 7:9-27; 8:13, 14; 9: 24-27:

Hebrews 1:3; 2:16, 17; 4:14-16; 8:1-5; 9:11-28; 10:19- 22:

Revelation 8:3-5; 11:19; 14:6, 7; 20:12; 14:12; 22:11, 12:

Notes:

Number 25: The Second Coming of Christ

The second coming of Christ is the blessed hope of the church, the grand climax of the gospel. The Saviour's coming will be literal, personal, visible, and worldwide. When He returns, the righteous dead will be resurrected, and together with the righteous living will be glorified and taken to heaven, but the unrighteous will die. The almost complete fulfilment of most lines of prophecy, together with the present condition of the world, indicates that Christ's coming is near. The time of that event has not been revealed, and we are therefore exhorted to be ready at all times.

Study and interpret the following verses:

Matthew 24:

Mark 13:

Luke 21:

John 14:1-3:

Acts 1:9-11:

1 Corinthians 15:51-54:

1 Thessalonians 4:13-18; 5:1-6:

2 Thessalonians 1:7-10; 2:8:

2 Timothy 3:1-5:

Titus 2:13:

Hebrews 9:28:

Revelation 1:7; 14:14-20; 19:11-21

Notes:

Number 26: Death and Resurrection

The wages of sin is death. But God, who alone is immortal, will grant eternal life to His redeemed. Until that day death is an unconscious state for all people. When Christ, who is our life, appears, the resurrected righteous and the living righteous will be glorified and caught up to meet their Lord. The second resurrection, the resurrection of the unrighteous, will take place a thousand years later.

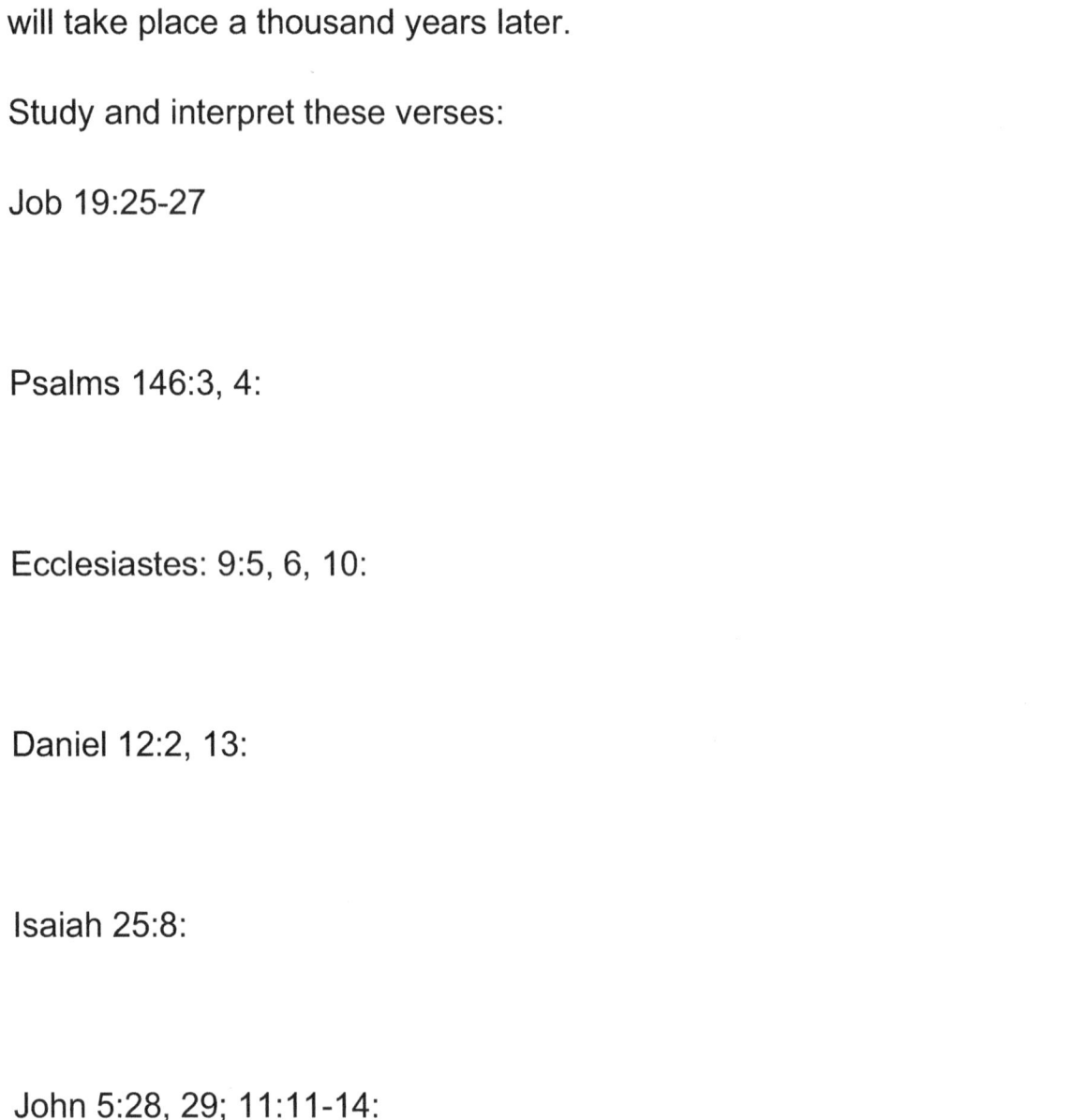

Study and interpret these verses:

Job 19:25-27

Psalms 146:3, 4:

Ecclesiastes: 9:5, 6, 10:

Daniel 12:2, 13:

Isaiah 25:8:

John 5:28, 29; 11:11-14:

Romans 6:23; 16:

1 Corinthians 15:51-54:

Colossense 3:4:

1 Thess. 4:13-17:

1 Timothy 6:15:

Revelation 20:1-10:

Notes:

Number 27: The Millennium and the end of Sin

The millennium is the thousand-year reign of Christ with His saints in heaven between the first and second resurrections. During this time the wicked dead will be judged; the earth will be utterly desolate, without living human inhabitants, but occupied by Satan and his angels. At its close Christ with His saints and the Holy City will descend from heaven to earth. The unrighteous dead will then be resurrected, and with Satan and his angels will surround the city; but fire from God will consume them and cleanse the earth. The universe will thus be freed of sin and sinners forever.

Study and interpret these verses:

Jeremiah 4:23-26:

Ezekiel 28:18, 19:

Malachi 4:1:

1 Corinthians 6:2, 3:

Revelation 20; 21:1-5:

Notes:

Number 28: The New Earth

On the new earth, in which righteousness dwells, God will provide an eternal home for the redeemed and a perfect environment for everlasting life, love, joy, and learning in His presence. For here God Himself will dwell with His people, and suffering and death will have passed away. The great controversy will be ended, and sin will be no more. All things, animate and inanimate, will declare that God is love; and He shall reign forever. Amen.

Study and interpret the following verses:

Isaiah 35; 65:17-25:

Matthew 5:5:

2 Peter 3:13:

Rev. 11:15; 21:1-7; 22:1-5:

Notes:

Made in the USA
Columbia, SC
26 July 2025